TRICKS AND TIPS

for experienced players

by Chris Raftis

C.R.Billiards,
P.O.Box 02903
Detroit, MI.
48202

Certified Instructor-Entry Level
by the Billiard Congress of America
for the 1992-1993 season

RAFTIS, Christos E., 1930-

Tricks and Tips for advanced players

1. Sport   2. Billiards   3. Pool (Game) 1. Title

Cover design by David Eleazar Mills

Published by: C.R. Billiards, P.O. Box 02903,
Detroit, MI. 48202

ISBN: 1-880135-02-7

CONTENTS

A BRIEF BIOGRAPHY

Born March 1st, 1930 in Indianapolis, Indiana. Relocated as an infant to Detroit, Michigan in 1930. Lived on the east side of Detroit for at least seven years and relocated back to Indianapolis. Attended James Whitcomb Riley School in Indianapolis until approximately age twelve when I relocated with my mother to Mitchell, Indiana (my mother's birthplace and the home of her relatives). Attended school in Mitchell until graduation from High School in May of 1948 when I rejoined my father in Detroit and started employment.

In the billiards world I was a teenage star. I started playing by invitation in 1944 and after several months became a proficient player. In 1945 I was able to compete against all comers at snooker and money ball. In 1946 at the age of sixteen I became a house man for Lowell Isom's City Pool Room located on main street in Mitchell, Indiana. I played for the house and managed the billiards room of six tables. My salary was fifty dollars a week plus fifty per cent of my winnings. Sometimes I would win fifty or more dollars in an afternoon's play. Money ball was the most popular game and the front table had the best players and the biggest bet. I have been a front table player since the age of fifteen. Currently I hold the National Veterans Eight Ball Championship title having defeated a field of fifty four contestants in October, 1991 at St. Petersburg, Florida.

A few special contests are notable: in 1950 I defeated Jake Ankrom, a five times national champion in match play at three cushion billiards; in 1951 I defeated Jean La Rue, the proclaimed world's one armed champion at American snooker by six hundred and thirty points in one afternoon; in 1963 I defeated the World's all around champion, Eddie (the Knoxville Bear) Taylor at jacked up nine ball competition by eleven games to six in Dayton, Ohio.

Improve Your Dead Ball Hits

by practicing the following:

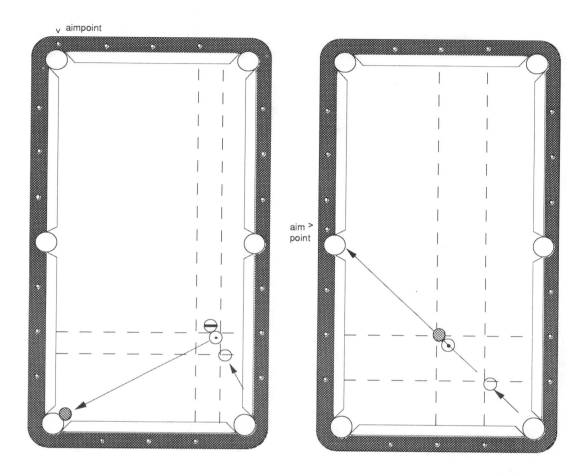

Place the balls in position as shown. Align the cue stick through the center of the cue ball and in line with the aim point. Strike the cue ball at the junction of the horizontal and vertical dividing lines. Employ a firm moderate stroke. Many beginners have a problem with this shot because they do not stay in position until after the follow through of the cue stick and also because there is a tendency to lift the cue tip from the table. Hold the cue level and follow through.

Exerpted from *Teach Yourself Pool* © 1991 Chris Raftis

Straight In Shots

Please practice the following:

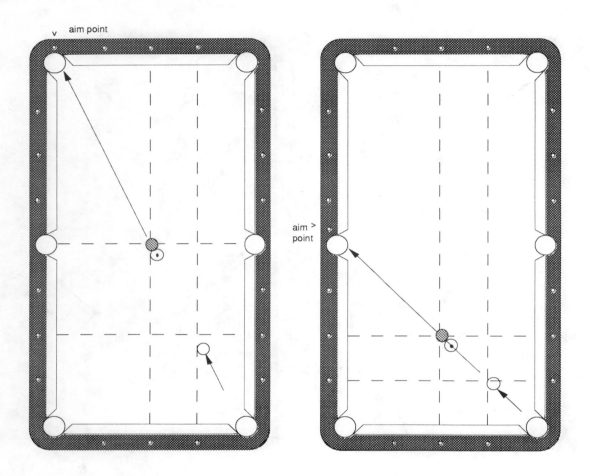

Place the balls in position as shown. Align the cue stick through the center of the cue ball and in line with the aim point. Strike the cue ball below the horizontal centerline of the cue ball while maintaining the alignment. Strike the cue ball with a firm soft stroke. If the object ball is straight in then you only have to aim the cue ball for the pocket and the object ball will automatically enter the pocket. Do not raise the cue tip when striking the cue ball.

Exerpted from *Teach Yourself Pool* © 1991 Chris Raftis

Shoot Straight Consistently

by practicing the following:

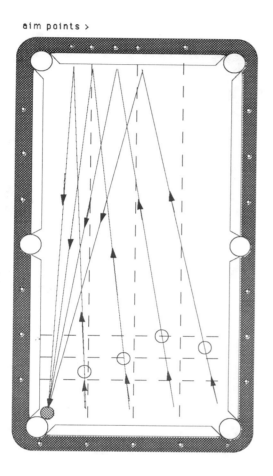

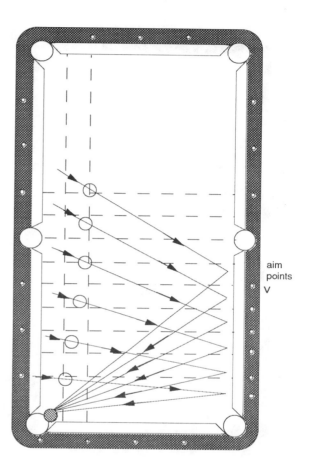

Place a ball on the table in position as illustrated. Strike the ball on the vertical center line (an imaginary line drawn from the top of the ball to the bottom of the ball dividing the ball in half). Strike as close to the horizontal center line as possible. One easy way to do this is to place the number on the ball at the imaginary junction of the horizontal and vertical dividing lines and then aim to strike the number. Use a force or striking power slightly in excess of what is necessary to reach the objective. It may be helpful to place an object, such as a piece of chalk or a piece of plastic on the rail as a sighting aid.

Exerpted from *Teach Yourself Pool* © 1991 Chris Raftis

Kick Shot Systems
Method of Computation

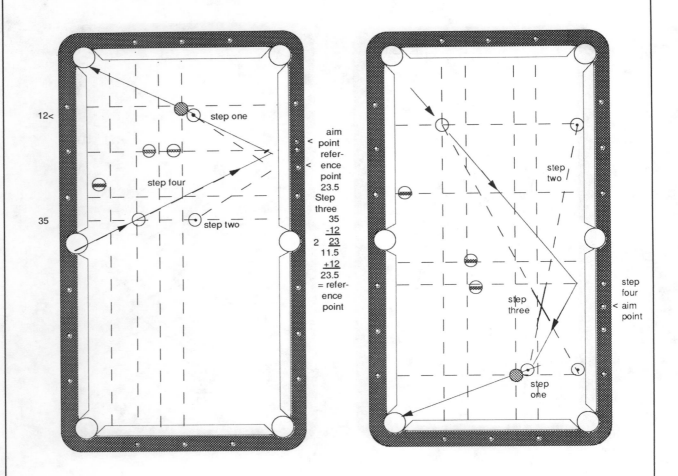

Place the balls in position as shown. Strike the cue ball in the center at the junction of the vertical and horizontal dividing lines. Strike the cue ball with a firm stroke while holding the cue level. The ball with the dot is a phantom cue ball. The computation for these shots can easily be facilitated by the use of a graph and phantom balls. If the entry angle is forty five degrees or thereabouts, then strike the cue ball in the center. If the entry angle is greater than forty five degrees, then strike the cue ball slightly below center. If less than forty five degrees, strike the cue ball slightly above center.

Exerpted from *Teach Yourself Pool* © 1991 Chris Raftis

Recognize Equal Angles
by practicing the following:

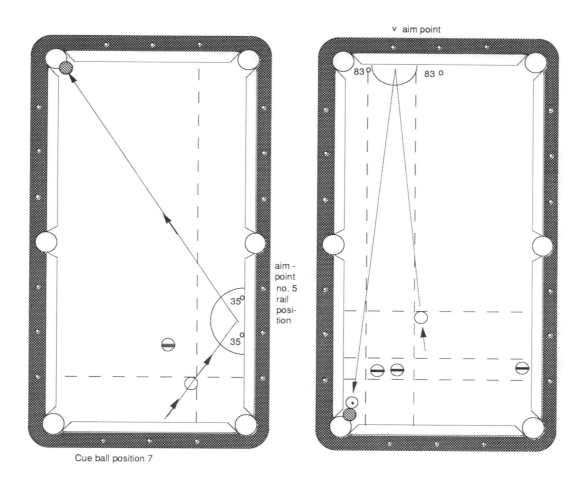

Cue ball position 7

Position the balls as shown. For the shot on the left strike the cue ball below the horizontal centerline and on the vertical centerline. For the shot on the right strike the cue ball at the junction of the horizontal and vertical centerlines. Always align the cue stick through the center of the cue ball and in line with the aim point before striking the cue ball. Strike the cue ball with a firm moderate stroke so that the cue ball will travel to a point just past the objective.

Exerpted from *Teach Yourself Pool* © 1991 Chris Raftis

Practice Kicks Using English

to improve your pool game.

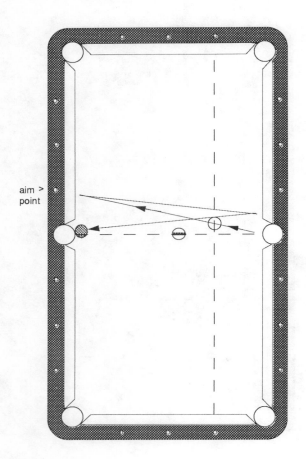
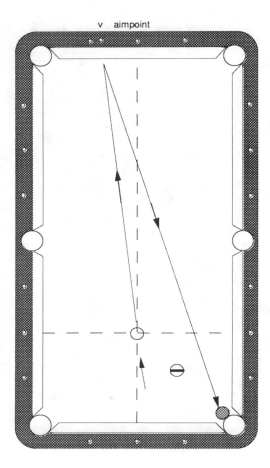

Place the balls in position as shown. Align the cue stick through the center of the cue ball and in line with the aim point. Now parallel that line of aim in order to strike the cue ball below the horizontal dividing line and for the diagram on the left to the left of the vertical dividing line and for the diagram on the right to the right of the vertical dividing line. Strike the cue ball with a firm moderate stroke. The objective is to draw the cue ball off the rail. Take the longest follow through possible.

Exerpted from *Teach Yourself Pool* © 1991 Chris Raftis

The Half Ball Hit

to be practiced as follows:

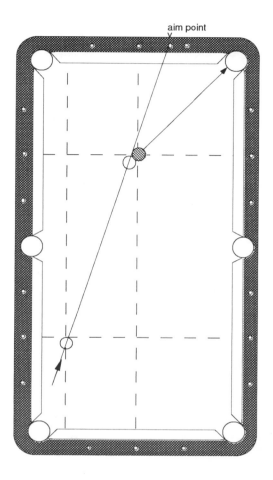
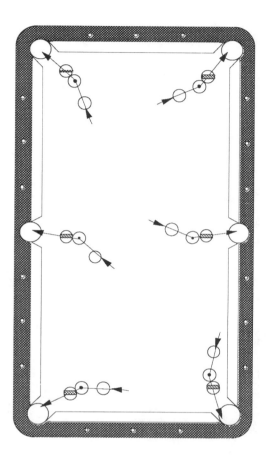

Place the balls in position as shown. Align the center of the cue stick through the center of the cue ball and in line with the edge of the object ball. Strike the cue ball above the horizontal dividing line and slightly to the left of the vertical for the shot on the left. Short shots like those on the right do not require off center hits. All of the shots on the right are the same half ball hit only they appear different due to positioning. Strike the cue ball with sufficient force to make the shot.

Exerpted from *Teach Yourself Pool* © 1991 Chris Raftis

Improve Your ¾ Ball Hits

by practicing the following:

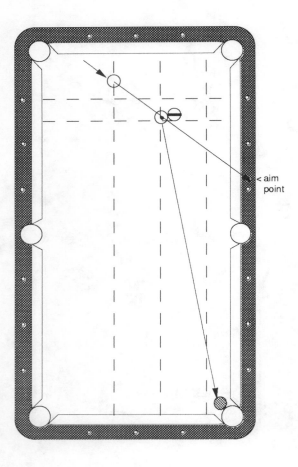
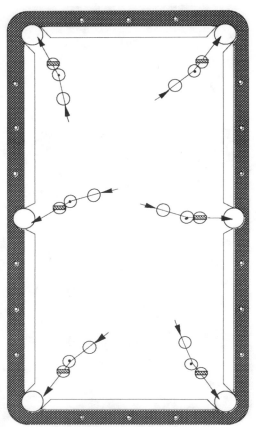

Place the balls in position as shown. Align the cue stick through the center of the cue ball and in line with the aim point. Strike the cue ball one cue tip above the horizontal dividing line and on the vertical dividing line. Employ a firm stroke. The diagram on the right is the same shot set up in different positions. Sometimes looks can be deceiving and by placing the balls in the same shot pattern although in different positions, one may conquer the deception and become an educated pool player. Be careful to insure the correct pocket entry.

Exerpted from *Teach Yourself Pool* © 1991 Chris Raftis

Improve Your 1/3 Ball Hits

by practicing the following:

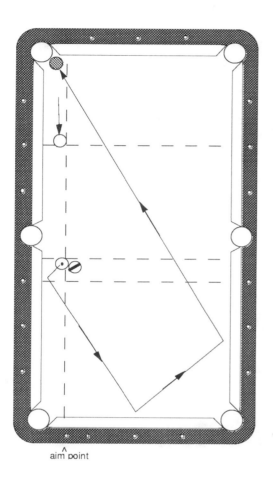

aim point

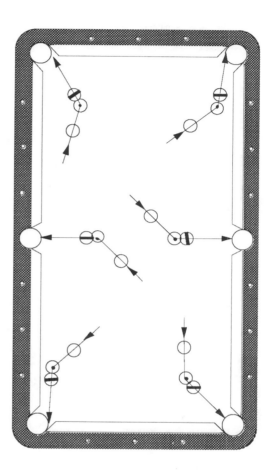

Place the balls in position as shown. Align the cue tip with the aim point. Parallel the line of aim in order to strike the cue ball one cue tip to the left of the vertical centerline and one half of a cue tip below the horizontal center line for the diagram on the left. Use a moderate force or force five. For the diagram on the right use a soft force or force one. Each force number indicates the distance a ball will travel on the table bed. Number one is one half the length of the table; number two one full length of the table; etc.

Exerpted from *Teach Yourself Pool* © 1991 Chris Raftis

Computing Object Ball Cuts
by practicing the following:

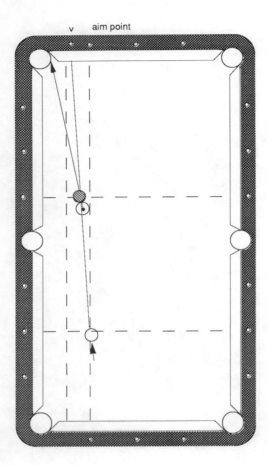
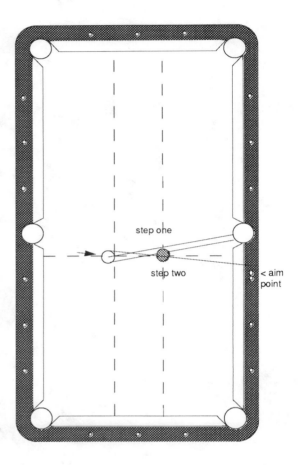

Place the balls in position as shown. The situation in these examples is that the object ball blocks the full view of the cue ball for the pocket. Examine the shot by determining what portion of the object ball is outside the line of the cue ball for the pocket entry. Now adjust your viewpoint so that the same portion of the object ball is outside the line of sight on the opposite side. This computation is only possible when the object ball obstructs the cue ball path.

Exerpted from *Teach Yourself Pool* © 1991 Chris Raftis

Effective Follow Shots

by practicing the following:

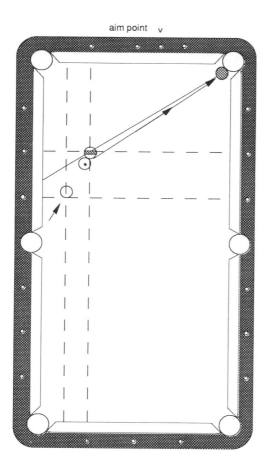
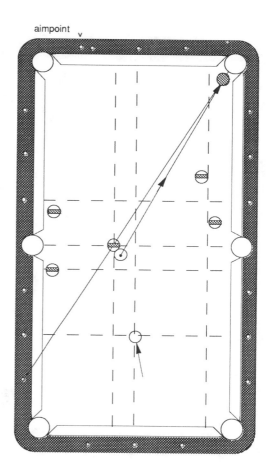

Place the balls in position as shown. Align the cue stick through the center of the cue ball and in line with the aim point. Strike the cue ball one cue tip above the horizontal dividing line of the cue ball and on the vertical dividing line. Employ a firm moderate stroke. The diagrams show a line drawn from the center of the object ball through the center of an obstructing ball. The alignment point for the cue stick is where that line contacts the surface of the obstructing ball.

Exerpted from *Teach Yourself Pool* © 1991 Chris Raftis

Draw Shots Made Easy

by practicing the following:

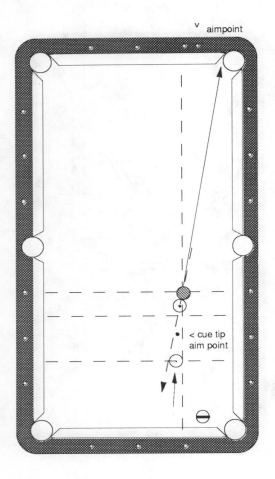

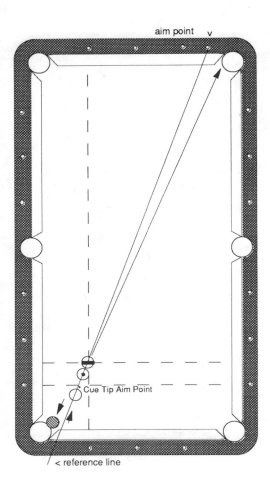

Place the balls in position as shown. Make a fist with your bridge hand. Place your fist on the table in line with the shot pattern and with the palm touching the cloth. Place the cue stick between your thumb and index finger. Align the cue stick below the horizontal center of the cue ball and on the vertical centerline. Strike the cue ball with a moderate stroke. Try to press the cue tip through the cue ball and onto the cloth at the reference shown. A quick wrist movement helps facilitate the draw. Remove your bridge hand quickly after the short follow through.

Exerpted from *Teach Yourself Pool* © 1991 Chris Raftis

Start Making Kiss Shots
by practicing the following:

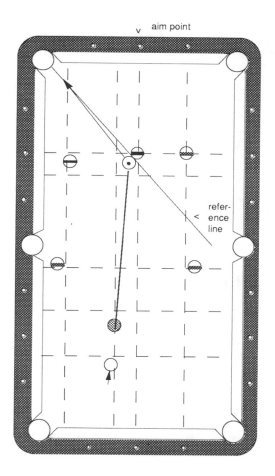
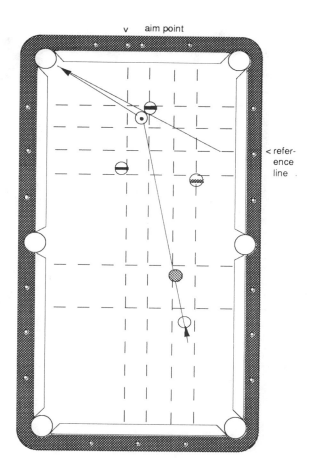

Place the balls in position as shown. To determine where and how the first object ball or the black ball must strike the second object ball or the striped ball, you need to know the location of the pocket in relation to the reference line or a line drawn tangent to the second object ball and the entry path of the first object ball into the pocket. For the diagram on the left you would strike the cue ball below the horizontal centerline and on the vertical centerline. For the diagram on the right you would strike the cue ball in the center.

Exerpted from *Teach Yourself Pool* © 1991 Chris Raftis

Easy One Rail Banks
by practicing the following:

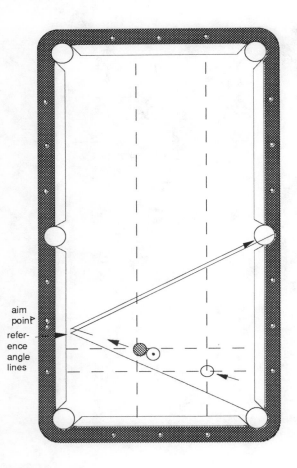

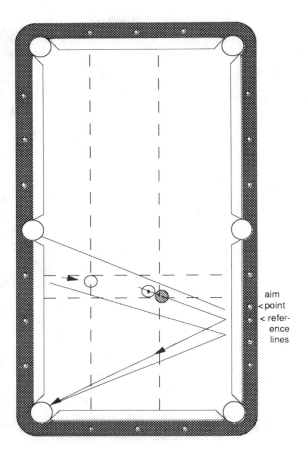

Place the balls in position as shown. Align the cue stick through the center of the cue ball and in line with the aim point. Strike the cue ball in the center at the junction of the vertical and horizontal dividing lines. Strike the cue ball with a firm soft stroke. Hold the cue level and leave the cue stick on the table after striking the cue ball. By using reference lines and reference angles the object ball path can be determined. The aim point is determined by drawing a line through the center of the cue ball and the phantom cue ball.

Exerpted from *Teach Yourself Pool* © 1991 Chris Raftis

Make More Two Rail Banks
by practicing the following:

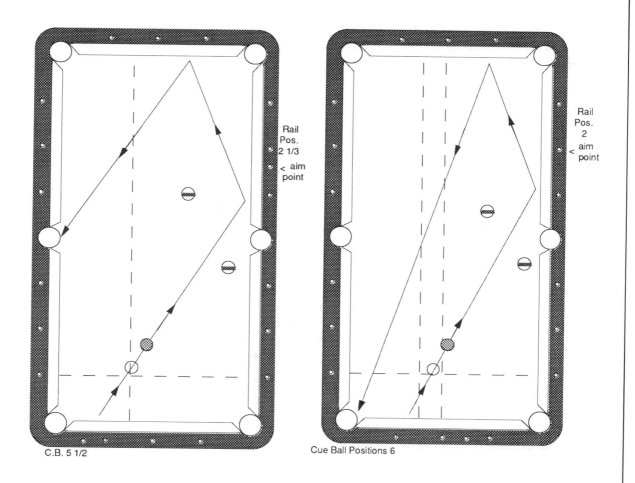

Place the balls in position as shown. Align the cue stick through the center of the cue ball and in line with the aim point. For the shot on the left strike the cue ball at the junction of the horizontal and vertical dividing lines. Use a firm hard stroke. For the shot on the right strike the cue ball on the horizontal dividing line and to the right of the vertical dividing line by one cue tip or one half inch. Strike the cue ball with a firm moderate stroke. Every table is an individual entity and has some variables. A slight adjustment may be necessary.

Exerpted from *Teach Yourself Pool* © 1991 Chris Raftis

Improve Your 3-Rail Banks

by practicing the following:

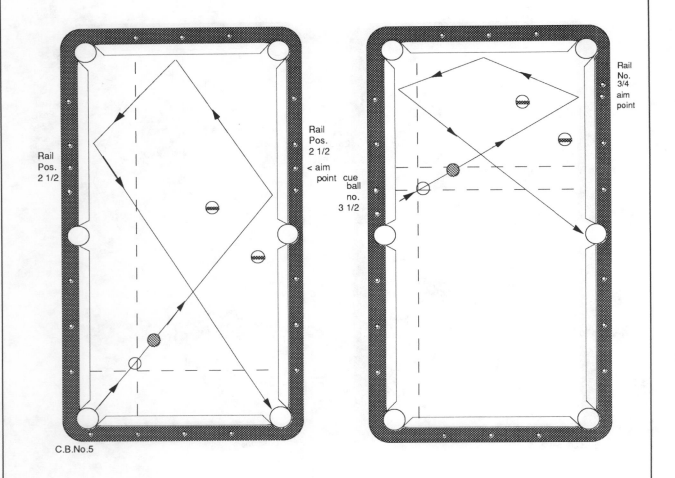

Place the balls in position as shown. Align the cue stick through the center of the cue ball and in line with the aim point. Strike the cue ball at the junction of the horizontal and vertical dividing lines. Use a firm moderate stroke. Hold the cue level and maintain your body posture until after the object ball strikes the first cushion. If you have struck the cue ball properly it will stop upon contact with the object ball and impart the major force to the object ball. The aim point may vary slightly due to the playability of the rubber cushions.

Exerpted from *Teach Yourself Pool* © 1991 Chris Raftis

Improve Your Rail Banks
by practicing the following:

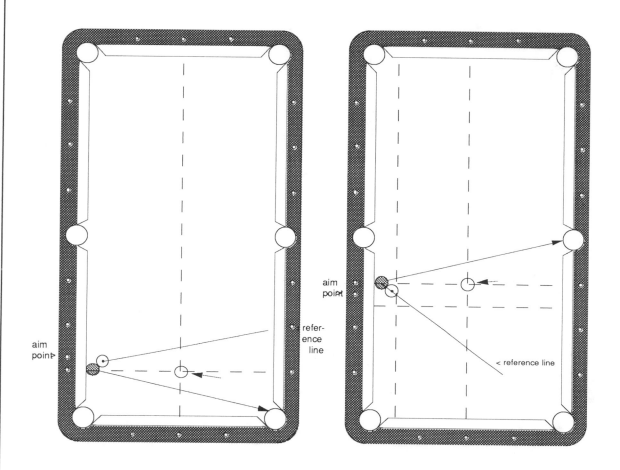

Place the balls in position as shown. The objective on these shots is to avoid a "double kiss" or in other words to avoid the cue ball striking the object ball twice resulting in a miss. So we will overcut the object ball and use reverse english on the cue ball which will influence the object ball towards the pocket. Strike the cue ball below the horizontal centerline for both shots. The shot on the left requires striking the cue ball to the left of the vertical centerline and the shot on the right requires striking the cue ball to the right of the vertical centerline. Use a firm moderate stroke.

Exerpted from *Teach Yourself Pool* © 1991 Chris Raftis

Throw Shot Examples

Practice the following:

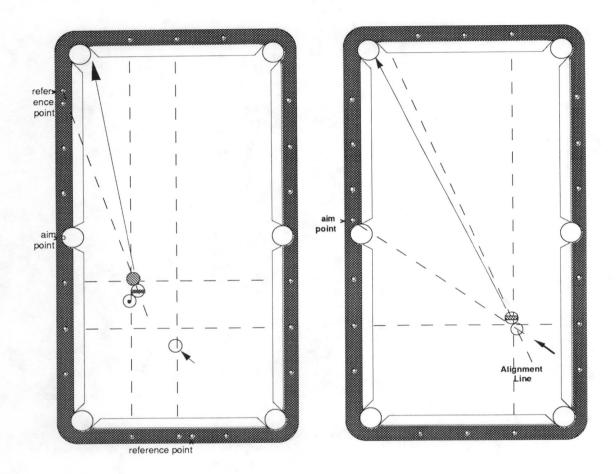

Place the balls in positon as shown. The ball with a dot is a phantom cue ball or the cue ball when it is in contact with the object ball. Align the cue stick through the center of the cue ball and in line with the aim point. For the diagram on the left parallel that line of aim in order to strike the cue ball below the horizontal center and to the left of the vertical centerline by one and one half cue tips or three quarters of an inch. The object ball will follow the straight line path.

Exerpted from *Teach Yourself Pool* © 1991 Chris Raftis

Set Shot Practice Shots

Set up and practice the following:

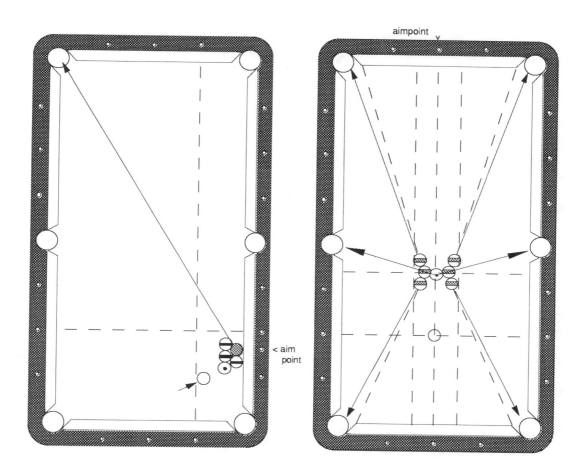

Place the balls in position as shown. Use the cue ball to tap the balls into position. For the left hand diagram tap the black ball first into position. For the right hand diagram tap the two center balls into position first but before tapping place a phantom cue ball to insure proper alignment of the two balls for the side pockets. Align the cue stick through the center of the cue ball and in line with the aim point. For the diagram on the left strike the cue ball in the center and for the diagram on the right strike the cue ball below the horizontal center.

Exerpted from *Teach Yourself Pool* © 1991 Chris Raftis

Manufacturing Shots
by utilizing the Diamond System

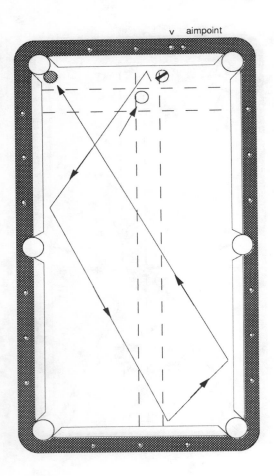
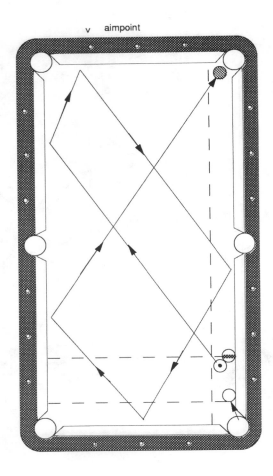

Place the balls in position as shown. Align the cue stick through the center of the cue ball and in line with the aim point. Parallel that line of aim in order to strike the cue ball below the horizontal dividing line one cue tip and to the left of the vertical dividing line one cue tip for the shot on the left and one half cue tip below the horizontal dividing line and one and one half cue tips to the right of the vertical dividing line for the shot pattern on the right. Strike the cue ball with a hard stroke.

Exerpted from *Teach Yourself Pool* © 1991 Chris Raftis

Here Comes The Spinner

Improve your spin shots by practicing the following:

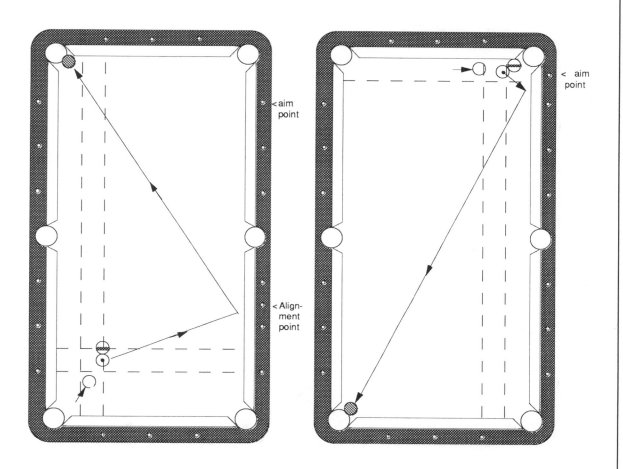

Place the balls in position as shown. Align the cue stick through the center of the cue ball and in line with the aim point. Parallel that line of aim to strike the cue ball one and one half cue tips from the vertical centerline for both shots. For the shot on the left strike on the left and one and one half cue tips above the horizontal dividing line. For the shot on the right strike on the right and one cue tip below the horizontal dividing line. Employ a firm moderate stroke to take the cue ball past the objective.

Exerpted from *Teach Yourself Pool* © 1991 Chris Raftis

Banks Using Imparted Spin

Please practice the following:

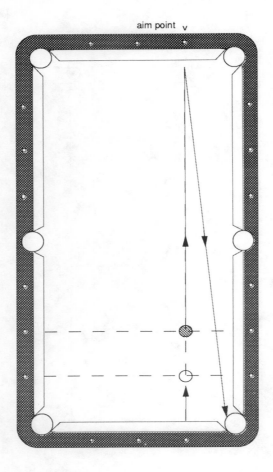
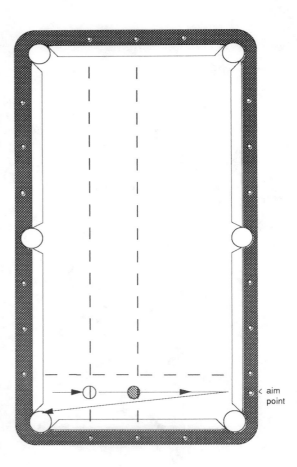

Place the balls in position as shown. Align the cue stick through the center of the cue ball and in line with the aim point. Next parallel the line of aim by moving the cue stick to the left of the vertical center line two and one half cue tips or three fourths of an inch. Keep the cue stick on the horizontal dividing line of the cue ball. Strike the cue ball with a force sufficient for the object ball to travel just past the pocket opening. The cue ball spin or "english" transfers to the object ball on this shot pattern.

Exerpted from *Teach Yourself Pool* © 1991 Chris Raftis

Successful Break Shots
by practicing the following:

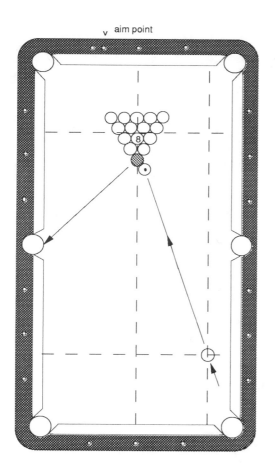
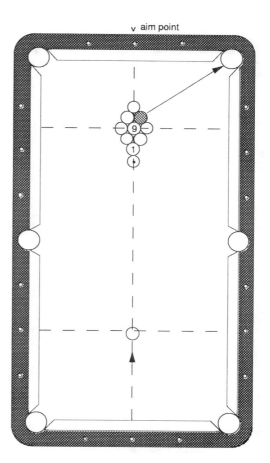

Rack the balls and place the cue ball in position as shown. Notice the ball with the dot which is the phantom cue ball or the cue ball in contact with the object ball. The shot on the left is played by striking the cue ball above the horizontal center and slightly to the left. The shot on the right is played by striking the cue ball below the horizontal center and as far to the left of the vertical that is practical. Strike the cue ball hard. Keep the cue stick level.

Exerpted from *Teach Yourself Pool* © 1991 Chris Raftis

The Diamond System
Two Rail Kicks

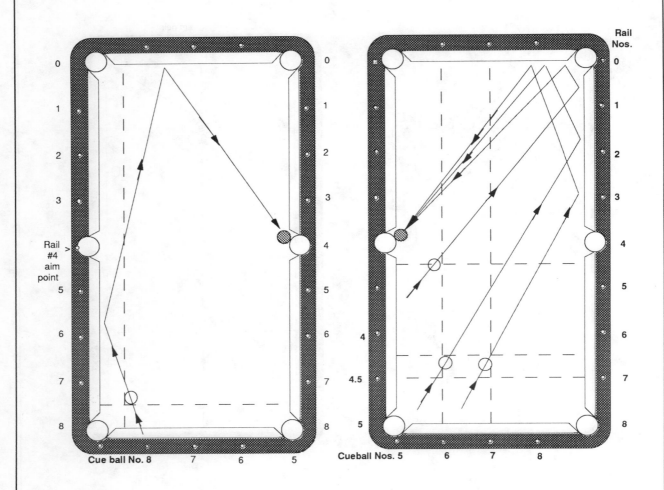

Because the playing surface of the table is twice as long as it is wide, a diamond system can be established. The objective illustrated is to reach rail positon four with the cue ball. On angles of entry greater than forty five degrees, strike the cue ball slightly below the horizontal centerline. On angles of forty five degrees or thereabouts, strike the cue ball at the junction of the horizontal and vertical dividing lines. By subtracting the desired contact position on the second rail from the cue ball position we arrive at the aim point on the first rail.

Exerpted from *Teach Yourself Pool* © 1991 Chris Raftis

The Diamond System
Three Rail Kicks

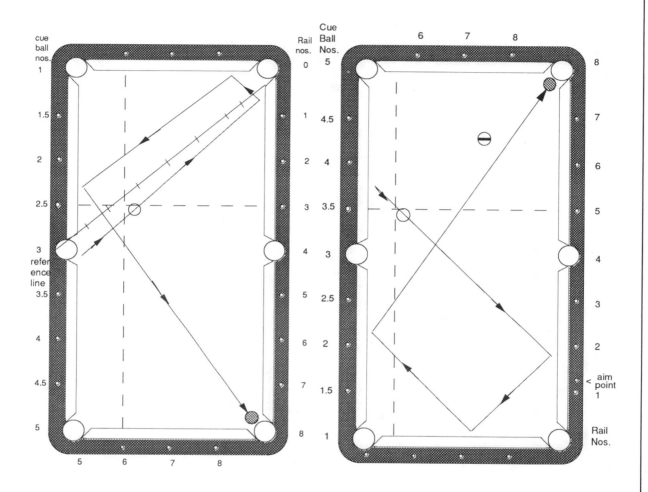

Because the playing surface of the table is twice as long as it is wide, a diamond system can be established. The objective in these diagrams is to determine the third rail contact point. On short angles it is three; on long angles it is two; and on medium angles it is two and one half. There may be a slight adjustment problem depending on the consistency and depth of the rubber cushion. By subtracting the third rail contact positon from the cue ball position, we arrive at the aim point for the first rail contact.

Exerpted from *Teach Yourself Pool* © 1991 Chris Raftis

Diamond System Naturals

showing the long, medium & short angles

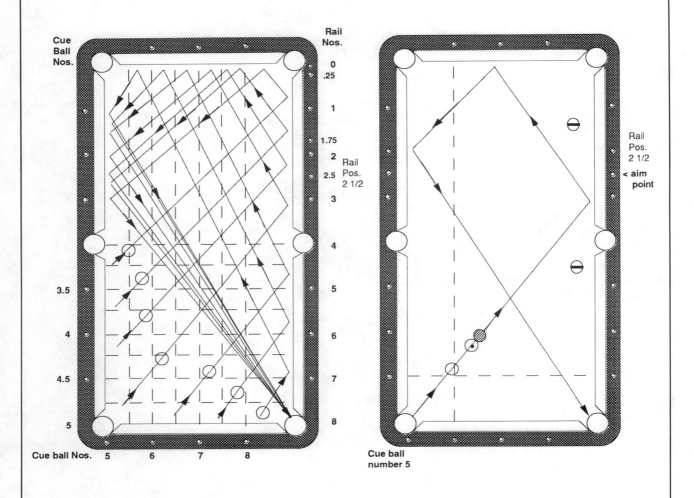

Place the balls in position as shown. Strike the cue ball at the junction of the horizontal and vertical dividing lines of the cue ball or in other words the center of the cue ball. The force of the shot or the speed imparted to the cue ball should be five or enough force to drive the cue ball two and one half lengths of the table. The diagram on the left shows the long angle into the corner coming into the third rail at diamond number 2; the medium angle into the corner coming into the third rail at diamond number 2.5; and the short angle into the corner coming into the third rail at diamond number 3. The position of the numbers and the angles need to be committed to memory. The diagram on the right shows how to use the system to produce bank shots.

Exerpted from Teach Yourself Pool © 1991 Chris Raftis

Improve Your Rail Cuts

by practicing the following:

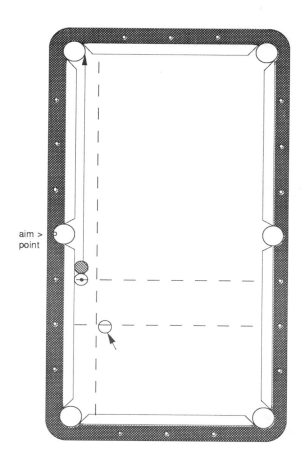
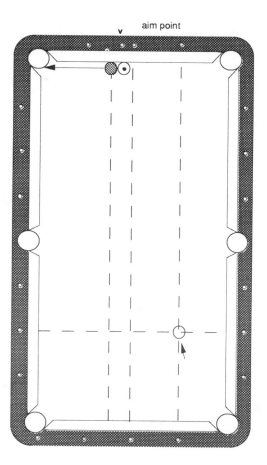

Place the balls in position as shown. Align the cue stick through the cue ball and in line with the aim point. For the shot on the left strike the cue ball below the horizontal centerline and to the left of the vertical centerline. The object is to divide the space between the object ball and the rail and align the centerline of the cue at the center point of that division. For the shot on the right strike the cue ball above the horizontal centerline and to the left of the vertical centerline. The object is to strike the rail in front of the object ball and to kick the object ball into the pocket.

Exerpted from *Teach Yourself Pool* © 1991 Chris Raftis